Mrs. Money Baggs Presents:

The Millennial Money Guide

Nicolle Williams

Mrs. Money Baggs Presents:
The Millennial Money Guide
Copyright © 2019 by Nicolle Williams

All rights reserved. No part of this publication may be reproduced, distributed, or transmitted in any form or by any means, including photocopying, recording, or other electronic or mechanical methods, without the prior written permission of the author, except in the case of brief quotations embodied in critical reviews and certain other non-commercial uses permitted by copyright law.

Hu(gh)man Publishing
www.hughmanpublishing.com

ISBN
978-0-2288-0463-5 (Paperback)

Table of Contents

Introduction Why Millennial Money Guide 3

Mrs. Money Baggs 7

Understanding Your Relationship with Money 11

    What's your money blueprint? 11

    Step 1 (AWARENESS) 18

    Step 2 (ACCEPT IT, FORGIVE, AND MOVE ON) 19

    Step 3 (ALLOW CHANGE) 20

    Step 4 (STICK TO IT) 21

My Introduction to Money (So, how did I learn about money?) 23

    How my introduction to money may help you 23

    Saving and paying yourself first 25

    Additional types of budgets 28

My Credit Lessons 31

    How credit can make or break you 31

    Credit is like your adult report card 34

    Are you thinking about improving your credit? ... 36

Net Worth 39

What is your net worth and where do you start?...39

Got Debt? 51

    Guess what, you're not alone. 51

Time to Save 57

    Invest your "coins" and build your own

    "money bag" 57

    Millennial Money Journal Activity 59

Millennials and Real Estate...61

    Homeowner at 21. What?..61

You'd Better Know Your Why 69

    What will keep you motivated?............................. 69

Stay on Course 73

    How to remain motivated and stick to your plan ...73

Conclusion 77

Acknowledgements

I want to thank you for your purchase. I know in today's content dense society, you have so many options, but you decided to rock with me, and I appreciate that.

I want to take this time to show gratitude for all the key moments that played a major part in moulding me into the woman I am today. I am blessed beyond words and know that I am the sum of all the experiences that have led me to this exact point.

Thank you Glendower Circuit/Galloway Glen, St. Martin de Porress, Ms. Kelly, Ms. Dias, The Honourable Lincoln Alexander, Marlene Ashman, Edith Blake, Mr. Class One, J Lee, Jacqueline Onassis, Canada Mortgage Network, Toronto Mortgage Man, Alexis Harris, Sean Liburd, Laideen Dockery, Reverend Olu and Vicki David, Ms. Brown (Grandma), HU(gh)MAN…one day I pray that I will be able to explore how all of these people/places have impacted me so deeply but for now I salute you.

To Sharon Stone — My mother and backbone and the person who makes all that I do possible. Mommy, I love you! Big up, Sharon Stone, *anywey she deh*!

Mikey — My Star Boy, My Young King, my young Usain — Thank you for teaching Mommy the power of dreaming and goal setting.

Jazzy — My Flower and Queen, thank you for teaching me patience and love. You keep me super grounded and fill me with lots of love and light.

Tay — My Boss, a true leader and the improved version (with all the kinks and adjustments removed) of me. She walks to the drum of her own beat; she isn't easily swayed, and she is loved and celebrated wherever she goes.

Mommy loves you guys and you are all the best version of me and an offering to this world. Remember always to be loving and kind to everyone (no matter). Always choose love. Xx

Atiba — My lover, friend, business partner, and SSS. I thank God for you daily. I love you more today than I did yesterday. We literally raised each other, and there is no one else in the world I would prefer to be on this journey with. Thank you for believing in me when sometimes I don't even believe in myself. For anyone who doesn't know, I may be the glitter, but Atiba is the one who makes me shine, he is always playing from the cut and he loves it. Thank you for riding with me through it all. There's no me without you. Xo

Introduction Why Millennial Money Guide

It's true there are tons of books already written on the subject of money and personal finance. I should know as I've probably read them all. I say this because, as the saying goes, nothing is new under the sun, but what I do know is that none of the current money books speak directly to the money concerns of today's millennials as I know this millennial money guide will.

It is my goal to provide a clear and simple plan for today's millennials; that is, a plan delivered in a super easy to understand way and gives you financial knowledge without all the fluffy jargon of yesteryears. With ten plus years in the financial industry, I work closely with today's millennials, and I've seen up front which money tactics work and which have been less effective. This millennial money guide will discuss all the good, the bad, and everything in between when it comes to money because it is my thought that many of the existing books written are not written with the millennial audience in mind. We have essentially been presented with thoughts and ideas (although, all valid) that don't speak to the existing conditions millennials deal with today.

Today's millennials have been faced with changes in work environments a recent study based on a national survey of 1,000 professionals, completed by the Canadian Centre for Policy Alternatives (CCPA) found that "22 per cent (of millennials) are working in precarious situations characterized by contract work, part-time hours, unpredictable incomes and a lack of paid sick days"[1].

This differs from the employment conditions of many "baby boomers" who were considered to be "career employees" who had guaranteed salaries, pensions, sick pay and paid vacations.

Another economic area that many millennials are seemingly being challenged in is the area of home ownership/real estate. A Financial Post illustrates the contrast in the ratio of family income needed to purchase for today's millennials in 2017 versus baby boomers in 1976. They found that 4:1 baby boomers could afford the median home price in 1976 versus 10:1 millennials in 2017[2]. This doesn't mean that the dream of homeownership has been erased for today's millennials it just means they have to be a lot more creative and thoughtful when it comes to this particular goal.

I also find that many of today's "money gurus" look at millennials as a "spoiled and entitled" group that does nothing more than complain, play video games, and look to Mommy and Daddy to financially support them. I don't believe in this rhetoric as I work with many millennials who are desperately looking for means and

---

[1] Arif Jetha "For Millennials, employment is a public health challenge, U of T expert," University of Toronto, September 7, 2018, https://www.utoronto.ca/news/millennials-employment-public-health-challenge-u-t-expert

[2] Naomi Powell, "Millennial housing crisis? Turns out, its real and worse than you thought," Financial Post, June 7, 2018, https://www.business.financialpost.com/real-estate/millennial-housing-crisis-turns-out-its-real-and-worse-than-you-thought/amp

solutions to have the financial independence of their parents and generations before them.

The goal of this book isn't to give you unattainable pie in the sky goals or another unachievable checklist of things to do but rather to teach you foundational skills, such as savings and credit basics that have been proven to lay the groundwork to put you on the path to your financial success, for you to build your financial life.

I strongly suggest you use what works for you in this guide and disregard the rest because I realize not everything that I teach will work 100% of the time for everyone. We all have different paths, and what may have worked for me may not be appropriate for you. My request is that you remain open to the ideas, but if some ideas work and others don't, focus on what works. It's that simple!

If your goal is to see improvements in your overall financial story, then this book is for you. You will be richer a year from now, and your future self will thank you for taking the first step necessary in your financial turnaround. Consider this book your first investment toward a wealthier You, and as one Canadian bank says, "You're richer than you think." Now is the time for me to show you how.

Mrs. Money Baggs

a.k.a Nicolle Williams

I am Nicolle Williams. I'm affectionately called Mrs. Money Baggs by friends, colleagues, and clients. They all consider me the go-to person for all things personal finance. I remember the first time I was called Mrs. Money Baggs by one of my great friends, Ms. Onassis. Our conversation went something like this:

"Nik (another one of my nick names), so and so was asking me about something to do with money, and I said, 'Look, you're asking the wrong person. You need to call Mrs. Money Baggs.'" This was the first time I was called Mrs. Money Baggs, and from then on the name just stuck. So believe me when I say you are in great hands, and if you don't believe me, ask Ms. Onassis.

There was a time when I knew zero about money and never would have dreamed that I would have a successful career as a mortgage agent and money coach and be an authority on the subject of money. The truth is what I know now didn't happen overnight, and it took me walking the same path I'm about to teach you, for me to have the financial success that I know you, too, can achieve.

You see, I grew up like most middle class (borderline poverty stricken) kids in the late '80s and '90s in the Galloway neighbourhood of Scarborough, a suburb of Toronto. Where I grew up, everyone was from a similar economic background, so it was easy for me to neglect to see that my family consistently walked on the edge of poverty and homelessness until I was in high school.

Like I said, I grew up with kids in similar economic situations, and even when my family did venture out of our neighbourhood, it was like we had a mind of "us against them" and, therefore, whatever "they" had, we didn't want. On the odd chance we did, some of us were brave enough to take it (steal it).

In my household, we knew the money code (or should I say we were given a "money blueprint" term popularized by T Harv Ecker), consisting of not asking for anything, not wasting anything, and never speaking our family "business" in public (outside the family home). This included when we didn't have hot water in the house but had sixteen people living there, or if the bank had posted a power of sale notice on our front door, meaning we were about to be homeless (and growing up, I experienced all these situations), but none of this was anybody's business and we were raised to understand this from a very young age.

To say that my money blueprint was riddled with a "poverty mindset" from the beginning is an understatement. My environment and family helped to program in me a mindset of poverty, scarcity, and lack. But one thing for sure is that everything I witnessed during my childhood has set me up to become the success I am today. All of it gave me the sheer will and determination to develop a lifestyle that is contrary to what was a part of my childhood. I was raised by my single mother with the assistance of my grandmother and I'm blessed and thankful for them because they did the absolute best with what they had. I give my mother, grandmother, and God all praise because of how difficult some of those times were, I cannot even begin to fathom how we made it through we never went to bed hungry or lived without a roof over my head, so I know I'm blessed, and what I say is no knock to them because I know they did their best.

By the time I was in high school, I began to understand the concepts of poverty and the systematic oppression in the "cards of life" that my mother and grandmother had been dealt. Earlier on in life they never learned how to win the game of life because they were playing the game with a losing hand.

They were immigrants who knew they "wanted better" for their family but were not given the proper tools to understand the Canadian economic system it was difficult for them to amalgamate into a system that was never taught to them or believed to be "designed" for them. Being raised in this environment taught me that life was an uphill battle, especially financially for individuals being raised and growing in one of Canada's lower income communities.

Understanding Your Relationship with Money

What's your money blueprint?

So why is understanding your money blueprint important? Because what works in the subconscious mind can and often dictates what is experienced in our reality. This is similar to the "don't ask, don't waste" belief I grew up with. I was positioned to have a poverty mindset without even knowing I was being conditioned by it . oI would reiterate sayings like "money is the root of all evil" (I no longer believe this). I also had the mindset of "why save for later, when I can barely afford necessities right now?" (This is an example of a scarcity mentality, always afraid that things will run out). Our relationship with money is impacted by our emotional, familial, cultural, and socioeconomic conditions. Plus, many financial experts, including Dave Ramsey (an American author, financial educator and host of his popular syndicated show "The Dave Ramsey Show"), believe that personal finance and one's relationship to money is 80% behavioural and 20 % knowledge[3]. The truth is we know what to do, but we don't do it, and let's face it, our behaviours are only an aftermath of our subconscious mind.

    Do you truly believe you deserve wealth? Will you do what it takes to achieve the life you truly deserve, or will you be quick to find excuses to avoid the time and effort you know is needed to make a significant shift in your life?

---

[3] Dave Ramsey, The Total Money Makeover (Nashville, TN: Nelson Books, 2013), 3

When most people are asked if they believe they deserve wealth, you would be surprised by the number of people who say, "I don't want to be rich, I just want to be 'comfortable'"…Comfortable? What does that even mean? Well, I will tell you that, for most people, being comfortable equals living paycheque to paycheque and having their basic needs met, meaning it would be difficult to have enough to plan a family vacation, or even be ok should there be an unexpected change to the family income like job loss.

We need to recognize that the visible is always the result of the invisible, like author T. Harv Eker wrote in his famous book *Secrets of the Millionaire Mind*, "If you want to change the fruits, you will first have to change the roots. If you want to change the visible, you must first change the invisible.[4]" This simply means that how we treat and react to money always begins internally with how we see ourselves with money (subconsciously), especially the conditioning we've come to accept as being normal, but which, unfortunately, keeps us financially stagnant year after year.

This guide was written to push you out of your comfort zone and into the zone of greatness, into billionaire status, and we will first start with the "root" (our minds) by knowing and conditioning ourselves to believe we are worthy of financial success. I come from the thought of if someone else has done it, I, too, can do it.

"Success leaves clues," (Tony Robbins)… so be sure to follow the clues.

---

[4] T. Harv Eker, Secrets of the Millionaire Mind: Mastering the Inner Game of Wealth, (New York, NY: Harper Collins, 2005), 12

When you change your money blueprint, your thoughts about money will change. You will change your life and, in turn, begin to live the financial life you've always dreamed of. "We cannot solve our problems with the same level of thinking that created them," said Albert Einstein, meaning in order to solve a problem, you first have to realize you have one, and then from this realization you can consciously work at solving/fixing the problem.

Millennial Money Journal Activity

So, now you need to think about your own personal money blueprint, ask yourself the following questions as part of the Millennial Money Journal Activity.

1. What's your first memory of money? And how does it make you feel?
2. How did you get money when growing up?
3. What did you buy when you did have money?
4. What are your money concerns today? And why do you have them?
5. How did your household talk about money while you were growing up?
6. Were you uncomfortable around your peers because of your economic status?

Other questions to consider:

7. Do you worry about money running out, not having enough money, being in debt forever?

Then your financial mindset may be one of **FEAR.**

8. If you were never encouraged to talk about money, whether good or bad, and the idea of someone asking you how much you make puts you into a tailspin…

Then your financial mindset may be one of **ANXIETY.**

9. Were you the child of divorce and witnessed first hand your family's financial life change in the blink of an eye? Did this propel a sense of wanting to be financially independent and having the need to save, save, save because you were always fearful that at any time things could turn for the worst or things wouldn't stay good for too long?

Then your financial mindset may be one of **FRUGALITY**.

The bottom line is you need to shift any negative money mindsets to positive mindsets, removing all the negative that has been planted from childhood and further packed on by life experiences.

Examples of negative money mindsets are:

1. People who said to you, "Money is the root of all evil."
2. People who said to you, "The rich get richer and the poor get poorer."
3. People who said to you, "Money doesn't grow on trees."
4. People who said to you, "You have to work hard to make money."
5. People who said to you, "That's not for people like us."
6. People who said to you, "Not everyone can be rich."
7. People who said to you, "You can't be rich and spiritual."
8. People who said to you, "Money doesn't buy happiness."

And the key, is, you to believe what they say/said, and this is a part of your own everyday money vocabulary and the energy subconsciously you live with.

Examples of Positive Money Mindsets:

1. People who said to you, "You can achieve anything you want."
2. People who said to you, "You can be rich and happy."
3. People who said to you, "How can I afford it?" rather than "I can't afford it."

"I can't help the poor if I'm one of them; so, I got rich and gave back, to me that's the win/win." (Jay-Z)[5]

Once you discover how you relate to money, it will become easier to work on improving your mindset and truly building a financial life you will be proud of.

Like anything, until your mind is set for success, you will find it difficult to see any true progress in your financial life.

> "Change Your Mindset, Change Your Life." (William James)

The reality is your thinking and beliefs play crucial roles in determining the level of success you will have.

So, here are some easy daily activities to do to help improve your money mindset/blueprint.

---

[5] Shawn Carter, The Black Album. Roc-A-Fella Records, B0001528-02, 2003, Compact disc

Step 1 (AWARENESS)

We've already covered this step, which is awareness, understanding our existing "money blueprint," and recognizing when we are thinking things that are not conducive to our financial success.

It is important to first recognize our current subconscious thinking, as this will give you the framework needed to consciously move forward in creating the change you choose to seek for yourself.

Back to the analogy that T. Harv Ecker gave regarding the tree, "if you want to change the fruit, you will have to change the root." This simply means you need to get to the core of your beliefs and uproot anything that works contrary to the new financial life you are trying to create for yourself. We need to "change the root" (our mindset)/

Millennial Money Journal Activity

Write out two examples of positive money declarations you will speak to yourself (preferably while looking at yourself in the mirror) at least twice a day, once in the morning and once before you go to bed.

Write out your own declarations.

It is recommended that you commit these declarations to memory and repeat them throughout the day until they begin to replace all the negative things you have been conditioned to believe and accept about your financial self.

Start off with two declarations and as you master committing these to memory, you can add more to your declarations as necessary, until you've replaced all your negative internal thoughts (that are really sabotaging your financial growth).

Some examples of positive money declarations:

- The world is filled with an infinite supply, there is no shortage, I am deserving and equipped to be a billionaire.
- My mind is conditioned for success and as such my outer world experiences success…I am equipped and deserving of becoming a billionaire.

For some of you, reading the above statements will make you uncomfortable, and I would say good. Growth never comes from a place of comfort; it almost always comes from uncomfortable places.

The key is to keep repeating these new, positive money declarations even as they feel uncomfortable until you get to a point where you truly believe all that you declare, and the declarations become second nature to you.

I come from the camp of shoot for the stars and if you don't hit the stars at least you may land on the moon. Nothing is too grand. Remember I said before that success leaves clues, meaning that today there are self-made billionaires. It is not impossible for us to work towards that or a similar goal for ourselves.

Step 2 (ACCEPT IT, FORGIVE, AND MOVE ON)

You need to accept, forgive and move on; similar to my own personal story. There was a time I had to accept my childhood for what it was and accept I wasn't a "trust fund" child. Nothing in this world would change that.

So, the sooner I forgave my mother and realized she really did an amazing job, the sooner I would heal and move on from any disappointments or excuses I created internally for myself.

You will have to do the same, forgive your parents for not being in a position to give you all the desires of your little heart while growing up. Or you may be the totally opposite; your parents could afford all the luxuries of life, but you feel it robbed you from a sense of truly understanding who you are (without their financial "handouts), or they've given you shoes too big to fill. Either way, you need to accept your past for what it was, forgive and move on.

This may be uncomfortable but until you deal with and shed all the hurt and unconscious baggage from your past, you will not be able to move on to the success you deserve in your life today. How unfair is it to our future selves to be weighed down and burdened with unpacked issues from our past.

Step 3 (ALLOW CHANGE)

You can be aware, and even accept that your "money blueprint" needs to change, but until you allow for things to change and manifest new positive money attitudes, you will be on a rollercoaster that seems to have no end. The great thing is, perhaps, even unbeknownst to you, you've already begun allowing change into your financial life by simply investing in this book and allowing this guide to put you onto your new path of financial success.

Step 4 (STICK TO IT)

Once you've developed a money plan that makes sense for you and your lifestyle, you need to stick to it, adjusting as needed but never deviating from the Key Core Concepts that are covered later in the guide. Discipline is your friend; it will keep you on task and focused. Discipline is what you need to achieve all your financial goals and give you that financially LIT life you deserve.

You can redesign your relationship with money and create the financial life you deserve.

Cheers to a new, fresh start!

My Introduction to Money (So, how did I learn about money?)

How my introduction to money may help you

Well, my first introduction into savings came around the time I started my first "real job." (Yes, I've always hustled. I lived in Glendower, a low-income housing community in Toronto's east end. At 5 years old, I picked flowers and sold them to our neighbours as they came home from work. Hey, back then, my goal was to make money to buy ice cream, candy or any kind of treat. (Friends and I would even turn around and sell flowers to the homeowners we had picked the flowers from.) So, yes, I've always been an entrepreneur and had the mindset for sales, always looking for opportunity. I learned very early that NOTHING in life was free and when you want something, you need to hustle, and be "on" your business (constantly working/hustling), however big or small. This was a sure way of getting things done, and this spirit also let me know I had a knack for sales.

My first real job came when I was 15 years old at a shoe store as a sales associate (OK, I'm trying to make it sound soooooo fabulous but growing up, everyone laughed at the thought of me selling shoes and would even reference the store where Al Bundy worked at in the TV show *Married with Children*). Despite their laughter, this job was a necessity for me as my family did not have the means to provide simple things like bus fare for me travel to and from school, or for lunch, or toiletries, or even those latest shoes or clothes I wanted. As I said, there was no extra money and back to my family's money code, we knew the unspoken rule of not asking for anything because, let's face it, priorities were a roof over our heads and food in the fridge.

Would you believe me if I said I grew up with major periods (years) of never having cable TV (that would be the equivalent to not having internet today)? Shoutout to one of my friends who used to record *Martin*, *Living Single*, *In Living Color* (popular 90s shows) on VHS (yes, this was pre-DVD, Blue Ray, and even USB) for me every week, so I wouldn't totally be out of touch with what was happening. #FirstWorldProblems, right? So, when I say I had to get on my "grind," I truly mean it. The best thing is I loved the independence and discipline working had provided me, and I credit this for building my existing work ethic.

With my first part time job in tow, I met with my soon to be mother in law who happens to also be a financial advisor. She sat me down and explained the concept of "paying yourself first" and putting money away for emergencies. So, I signed up and she became my first financial advisor and I began my first savings. To say I fully understood all that she said or what I was invested in would be a lie but what that encounter did was lay the framework for building the discipline I needed to continue a life of "paying myself first," stowing money away for emergencies and having money to take advantage of opportunities (investments) that would come my way.

Saving and paying yourself first

According to Forbes millennials prioritize experiences over stuff[6] making it important that our money conversations match this new way of thinking and approach. Millennials want to invest in their "now" and don't want to compromise, so it is up to me to show you how to spend today without compromising your tomorrow. So, instead of me telling you what you can't do, I'm here to show you how much you *can* do.

The earlier you start this plan, the less you will have to compromise.

With these planned experiences, millennials are taking those exotic trips, buying that designer bag and driving those luxury cars that their parents thought were reserved for only the uber rich or for their retirement. This is no longer the case nor the way of thinking.

So, how do we ensure financial success while balancing living in the moment without sacrificing our futures? Well, I know budgeting and the old way of money management won't cut it for today's money times.

I know, I know, I know, I will probably get a ton of emails and calls for even suggesting that budgets are a thing of the past. Let's face it, budgets are too rigid and don't allow for any flexibility in one's situation. Truly similar to diets, they work for a small segment of individuals, but the majority don't notice any changes in behaviour. It has also been my experience that when working with clients and implementing budgets, when

---

[6] Ashley Stahl, "How Millennials Spend Their Money (Hint: Experiences Trump Possessions)", Forbes, Nov. 15, 2016, https://www.forbes.com/sites/ashleystahl/2016/11/15/how-millennials-spend-their-money-hint-experiences-trump-possessions/#1ccc4ccf5cfb

things don't go as planned many people feel riddled with a sense of failure and disappointment and instead of adjusting their budgets, I find that many people quit budgeting and return to their old routine of no plan or strategy. This leaves them with no savings or debt management strategy, and no action steps to encourage their financial success. Their inactions leaves them discouraged and disenfranchised from their personal finances and many take the approach of "hating to discuss or think about money.

When I was introduced to the Profit First Approach, coined by Mike Michalowicz in his book *Profit First*, it brought me back to the concept that I was first introduced to by my mother in law of paying yourself first. It was like a light bulb went off; then I began questioning why this method wasn't as successful as it should be. Especially for those trying to improve their financial situations and beginning to lay the foundation for building wealth habits. I know we've all heard the phrase pay yourself first but usually this concept is emphasized and worked into someone's budget. When people abandon their budget (usually because it is too rigid), they also abandon the brilliance and simplicity of the method of paying yourself first. This led me to the notion of the No-budget Budget (an oxymoron, I know, but work with me).

The No budget Budget does offer some structure but in a fluid way that still allows for flexibility without compromising the important factors needed for one to gain financial wealth and independence.

My No budget Budget adopts the system by Mike Michalowicz's Profit First System (essentially, paying yourself first). There are four accounts everyone starting off should have (for the sake of this book, I will refer to these accounts as "buckets").

Bucket A: Income Account. This account is for all deposits of employment and investment income.

Bucket B: Profit Account (long term savings account). This account is where you will begin to put aside a percentage of all your income. At this point, it is less important for the money to be invested but rather to direct it toward building the habit of saving. To ensure success, wherever possible make the deposits automatic to match the dates of income being deposited into the income (Bucket A) account.

Bucket C: Emergency Funds. I recommend that you put aside 3 months' worth of "fixed expenses" into this account as a cushion should an emergency arise.

Bucket D: Operating Account. This is the account that all your fixed expenses will come from, e.g. housing costs, debt repayment, cell phone/internet payments etc.

Bucket E: Variable Account. This variable account can be used to pay for all other variable expenses. So, guess what, whatever is left allows you to enjoy your lifestyle choice of now…so you want to take that trip? If the money is there, take it. You want to have that fancy dinner? If the money is there, have it.

This concept is beyond important for today's generation because we are living in a time of instant gratification and, as a result, everyone wants to enjoy the luxuries of life right away and not in retirement or in 15–20 years.

So, when you take your profit first (pay yourself first) by making savings automated and matching them with your income deposit dates, or if necessary, taking "profits" when income is received if you are a contractor worker or self employed. Ultimately you are building your wealth and staying within your means so you can enjoy your life on your own terms because the Variable Account bucket can be spent how you see fit.

I don't get so fixated on categories and on what is spent on what. As long as you are paying yourself first (saving) and have money for your needed fixed expenses, the remainder forms your variable account to spend how you see fit. So, if paying off debt is of high importance, you would use some funds to aggressively pay debt down. If travelling to that exotic island is important, do it. If buying that designer bag is important, do it, if you're saving for a major purchase such as a home, you can allocate the "variable" funds to that. The whole idea is that you have control to do what is important to you in that moment and, believe me, things change, so what's important today may not be important tomorrow. This no budget budget offers this flexibility.

For all of you who scoffed at the idea of having a no budget budget, I've included some popular budgeting systems in case the no budget budget system doesn't work for your lifestyle.

Additional types of budgets

1. Cash Diet — With this budget you will pay for everything in cash. You need to sit down and add up all of your income and subtract all fixed bills, subtract savings (long term and short term), then whatever is left is yours to spend as you see fit. You do this by carrying cash and once the cash is done, you stop all spending. Tip: Leave a $100 buffer for any items you may have forgotten.
2. Tracking Every Penny — You keep a meticulous record of everything you spend over the month. Some people record transactions and review them daily or weekly. This budget will only work if your diligent to record every single item

(including cash transactions). You can categorize your spending (food, housing, debt repayment etc.). You can even chart expenditures using an Excel spreadsheet or take advantage of one of the many available budgeting apps in either the Google Play or Apple store.
3. Envelope Budget — Similar to the cash diet, you would remove all your monthly income and allocate your spending categories into envelopes (or in today's modern society, specific accounts) designated for particular spending needs, e.g. an envelope for housing costs, an envelope for savings, an envelope for transportation, an envelope for entertainment, debt repayment etc. This allows for meticulous tracking and allows for you to pinpoint exactly what categories and items you are spending on, on a consistent basis, and should you need to eliminate something, it will be easy for you to pinpoint your spending patterns.

From here, it is all about putting your financial well being first, sticking to something that will work for your lifestyle, and being diligent to live your life by it day in and day out. If you find the budget style you started off with is no longer serving your needs, it is quite OK to switch to a different budgeting style. The key is to build the discipline from knowing that your future life and your financial freedom, deserves every ounce of effort you can give it today.

My Credit Lessons

How credit can make or break you

It's so funny when I think about one of my first experiences with credit. It was in my first three days at university, strolling the university hallways. I was bombarded by a young man probably three to four years older than me offering a free Toronto Raptors t-shirt if I signed up for the credit card he was pushing. I was like, *a free Raptors shirt just for signing up? Sure*…and that was it, the good people of MBNA approved my first $2,000 dollars in credit without explaining one thing to me, no phone call, no confirmation of employment but, voilà, credit for a young, inexperienced girl to go hit the mean streets with (I felt like I hit the lottery).

It would be years later that I would realize how destructive and exploitive this behaviour is by the credit card companies when I would see countless clients express their credit woes all from an experience similar to mine.

This is why until this day I am extremely thankful for the likes of Edith Blake, a lawyer I interned for while I was in university. (You see, I entered university with the desire of pursuing a career in law; this obviously all changed when I discovered my true passion in real estate and personal finance.)

Edith Blake was a real firecracker, and never one short with words, she would say what was on her mind and was very passionate about excellence, especially when pulling excellence out in other women in such a male dominated world.

You see, I had been working with Ms. Blake for a couple of months when she candidly said to me one day, "Nicolle, you always have the best clothes, your hair is always done…And I know when I was in university, I didn't have nice things as it appears you have." (At this time I was going to school full time, working part time and interning, un-paid, with Ms. Blake's law firm.) She called me into her office for a one to one conversation. As I was about to close the door, she told me to grab my bag, so I went to my desk to grab my Daniel Leather $300 bag. Then she said, "Let me see it." I looked at her quizzically, and she said, "Let me see the credit card."

I said, "Oh, it's just this MBNA card I got from school." As I pulled the card out, she proceeded to ask me what my credit limit was, how much I owed, what my interest rate was, when my billing cycle was, what my minimum payment was, and what my interest free grace period was. I was in complete shock because other than knowing my credit limit, I knew zero, zilch else. She explained that the goal of a credit card was to have access to the bank's money for free with that interest free grace period and to pay the balance in full once that period was up. She explained that anything outside of that was poor money management. She knew I had probably racked up a balance on the card, and now had the responsibility to get myself out of debt, and while I worked on that, I needed to maintain great credit by at least paying the minimum payment on time every month. This conversation was blowing my mind because up until this point, no one ever explained credit to me or explained what it meant to have good credit. Mind you, by this time, I had a student loan from the Royal Bank of Canada (RBC) as well as another credit card with a $500 limit, which was my first credit card with the same bank. I had met with an RBC advisor to arrange financing for my upcoming tuition, and once they approved my student loan (with no cosigner), they decided to throw in a "small" credit card—again, with no true explanation.

I obviously take responsibility for accepting these products, but when I think back on it, within weeks, I, a new university student at age 18, had debt in excess of $10,000 (inclusive of student loans and credit cards). This was beyond crazy, and what was crazier was that until Edith Blake sat me down that day, I had zero clue about anything credit (although, I kept swiping that card), but boy did I look fly!

So, you can imagine my horror when Ms. Blake told me she was giving me homework that evening. I was to go home, open my credit card statement, review all the terms and conditions (if I didn't have the terms and conditions, I should give the credit card company a call and request them) and when I returned the next week (I worked for her one day a week for a six hour shift), I should be able to answer all the questions she had originally posed to me that I could not originally answer.

When I got home that night, I delved right in and was shocked at how reckless I had been with spending without even knowing what the hell I was doing. But boy, was I happy for Ms. Blake. You see, if it had not been for her, I probably would have damaged my credit, delved further into debt and perhaps taken a different path in life. I took everything she said to heart and from that day on, I became obsessed with learning everything I could about money. Up to that point, I had been fixated on getting money and spending money (again, this goes back to my original money blueprint). As a child, although I always had a roof and food and everything else, I had to provide for myself as an adult. And let's be honest, I was raised in a culture where you wore your money (as stupid as that now seems to me) rather than using money as the tool it is.

Credit is like your adult report card

So, this backstory is to say that if no one has sat you down to explain credit, and you feel you've dug yourself into a hole, let me be the first one to say, you are not alone. The good thing is every day is a new opportunity to live, learn, and grow. The following are the credit tips I give all my clients looking to improve their overall credit situation.

First off, you must know where you stand, and that means, how do your creditors see you? Request a free copy of your credit file from both Equifax (www.equifax.ca) and Trans Union (www.transunion.ca). In Canada, these credit reporting agencies keep a record of your payment and credit history, and report to your existing and future creditors about how you maintain and pay your credit facilities. They keep both positive and negative history of your payments, credit usage/balance outstanding, collection items, bankruptcies etc., in some cases up to fourteen years for multiple bankruptcies and 10 years for judgements (all other history remains for shorter time frames depending on the province/territory you reside in and the type of history reported). The following play a role in determining a consumer's credit history and score:

35% of your credit is based on payment history
30% based on "utilization"
15% length of credit history
10% new credit
10% credit mix (types of credit accounts)

The above determine the range of poor credit to excellent credit. The obvious preference is for you to have excellent credit as determined by Equifax (the credit agency the majority of lenders use). A credit score is a three digit number ranging from 300–900 and act as a quick reference for, primarily, lenders and creditors to determine how comfortable they are in extending debt or going into business with a consumer. Credit scores below 580 fall in the "poor" credit range, scores from 580–669 are generally considered "fair", 670–749 credit is considered "good", and 750 and up is generally considered "excellent" credit[7]. Credit scores are based on the mix mentioned earlier, but it is important to mention that credit scores are often different between Equifax and Transunion as not all lenders report to both credit agencies, and there are different scoring models used from one agency to another (for the purpose of simplicity and since the majority of Canadian lenders use Equifax, the information provided is based on the scoring and reporting of Equifax).

The simplest way to have a positive credit report, and thus a positive credit score, is by establishing two active trade lines (credit facilities that you consistently use and are being reported as "active" on your credit file, e.g. credit cards, lines of credit, loans). When using credit cards, you could make one or two small purchases every month, keeping your balance to about 30% of your available credit (formally called "utilization", e.g. if you have a $1,000 credit card limit, don't spend more than $300), then pay your balance off in full every month, and then, like clockwork, you do it all over again. This is one of the sure ways to help you get an A1 credit score to put you on the path to credit gold status. It is important to note that credit plays a major role in our lives and can

---

[7] "What is a credit score", Equifax Canada, 2018, https://www.consumer.equifax.ca/personal/education/credit-score/what-is-a-credit-score/?CID=3&%2Bcredit%20%2Bscore%20%2Bcanada_M_p&adID=81707478482320&DS3_KIDS=p28939836842&msclkid=f79ab6cd49ac17c179c8ed2506420099&gclid=CPm_nO3YzN4CFaqIxQIdAlgLOw&gclsrc=ds

either propel us toward or hinder us from achieving some major financial/personal goals. The following are some examples of how credit plays a role in helping us achieve some of our goals, job prospects (most employers check the credit of potential new hires), car loans/personal loans (good credit versus poor credit could mean the difference in lower interest rates being offered by a lender, therefore, affecting monthly payments), rental applications (many landlords check the credit of a potential tenants), and eventual home purchases.

Once you have copies of your credit history, and you see where you stand, you can make a plan to help either improve your overall credit situation or maintain positive habits if your credit is in the "good/excellent" range.

Are you thinking about improving your credit?

Managing your credit is an important part of your present and future financial success. I've put together some tips for you:

- For all revolving credit balances, keep them at or below the 30% utilization rate, e.g. if your limit is $3,000, keep your spending balance below $900.
- Creditors do not like seeing patterns of missed and slow payments (where possible set up all credit on a pre-authorized payment plan, to ensure at least minimum payments are made on or before the due dates). If you are a contract worker, self employed or receiving irregular income and find it difficult to be on a pre-authorized payment plan, you'll have to ensure at least minimum payments are made, so set up reminders through your calendar app to be able

to meet these obligations. If you are finding it difficult to meet minimum payments because of the irregularity of your income, then it may be necessary for you consolidate all debts to better manage your credit. In that case, it is better to have one creditor rather than multiple lenders to have to pay monthly and therefore should ease the burden.

- With these payments all debt that has been written off or is in collection accounts needs to be settled and paid in full with the lenders (it will be extremely difficult getting a mortgage with outstanding collections, for example). I always recommend trying to settle for at least fifty cents on the dollar (e.g. if you owe $3,000, try to settle for $1,500) and ensure that when you call to negotiate your debts that you are in the position to pay out your settlement as many collection companies will only give you a couple of days to a couple of weeks, maybe, for you to make good on agreed terms or the settlement agreement can be voided.
- Also review all items on the credit report to ensure all debts are reflected correctly including credit limits and amounts outstanding.
- Be mindful of the number of inquiries you make (this includes when lenders request to review your credit file when you're trying to secure new debt/credit). It is recommended that you do not have more than three hard inquiries (when a creditor requests a copy of your credit file) in a 12 month rolling period. When you have more than three "hard inquiries", the impression given is that you are a credit "seeker", which often is an indication that you are not able to

manage your existing credit well or you do not have sufficient cash flow to manage your day to day living expenses.
- Have, at minimum, two active trade lines (credit facilities reporting on your credit bureau), preferably revolving credit, e.g. line of credit from a bank or a credit card (as credit card companies tend to have the biggest impact on credit increases). Having a mix of credit types shows potential lenders your ability to manage different types of credit and also shows them your credit maturity. Let's face it, the majority of people new to credit start off with a credit card, and the more established a person becomes with credit, the lending institutions (like CIBC or other "lender(s)") offer the consumer other products such as lines of credits, mortgages etc.

As a consumer, you may or may not want to expand your credit repertoire, or you may need to add a "trade line" here are two options I can recommend:

- Capital One Master card for their "credit rebuild card"
- Any major banks "secured credit card" option

Net Worth

What is your net worth and where do you start?

The simple definition of net worth is assets minus liabilities, for you to fully understand the meaning of "net worth" we would take all your fixed assets (property, vehicle(s) etc) as well as cash and cash-like instruments (assets that convert into cash quickly such as bonds, guaranteed investment certificates, money market accounts etc.) minus your liabilities (debts, loans, mortgages IOU's etc). The goal is to have a positive net worth when you complete this calculation. One of your biggest financial goals will be to have appreciating assets (investments that will grow in value year over year) that will help build your overall wealth. Some examples of assets that people invest in to appreciate or increase their net worth are real estate, the stock market, and tech and business start-ups, but in order to devise a long term strategy that may include these, it is important you work with a trusted financial advisor who takes a holistic approach to your overall finances.

So, instead of going into asset building strategies, I will highlight the key things to look for when hiring and working with a financial advisor.

Things to ask your potential financial advisor:

1. **Who is responsible for managing your money?** A lot of times financial advisors pick from pre-determined portfolios and invest their clients' money in these funds with little say from the clients about which funds are included in these portfolios. The advisor is actually more of

a middle man between the fund manager and you, the (in this case, it would be just as important to know information about both the fund manager and your investment/financial advisor).
2. **What is the advisor's background?** Many investment advisors have business and finance degrees and years of experience as investment analysts or traders at major financial firms. Ensure that these advisors are in good standing with no complaints or disciplinary actions registered against them.
3. **Who pays you?** Virtually all the compensation an investment advisor receives should come directly from his clients. Any other sources of income should be insignificant and fully disclosed. Brokers, on the other hand, can earn commissions on trades, trailer fees from mutual funds and annuities, and bonuses tied to their firm's proprietary investment products or trading.
4. **Are you always legally bound to act in your clients best interest?** The answer must be yes, all of the time. If it is, get it in writing. This is a fiduciary duty. A fiduciary is a person who holds a legal or ethical relationship of trust with one or more other parties (person or group of persons). It's a well established legal principle, backed by decades of precedent, to protect you the client.

By reviewing these questions, plus any other pertinent questions you have, you should be able to sift through the advisor pool to find someone suitable for you and your family. I always recommend that when you are looking to begin a new relationship with an advisor to always ask for referrals from family, friends or colleagues. A mere referral is not enough, but it is a good starting point to finding the right advisor for you.

A statistic that my good friend, who is also a financial advisor, likes to highlight is that a "household with an advisor for fifteen years or more, accumulates, on average, almost four times more assets than non advised households," it is also said that the "advised household saves at twice the rate of 'passive,' non advised households[8]."

There is an advisor available for every stage of one's financial life. Finding one is a matter of seeking out the best advisor for you and your family and forming a working relationship that will hold you accountable to achieving your financial dreams.

I'd like to note that for your household, you should establish your financial power team, specialists rather than generalists, to help you and your family achieve your financial dreams. Each team member has a specific role to play in assisting you in achieving your goals.

Your financial power team can be fluid; there may be times you lean on one specialist more than another, but at the end of the day, they all make invaluable team members. Some examples of your financial power team are:

Accountant/Bookkeeper
Lawyer
Financial Advisor/Insurance Advisor
Mortgage/Credit Specialist
Real Estate Agent
Banker/Account Manager

The goal of building your net worth is to see an improvement, year over year, from where you stand.

---

[8] Jon Cockerline, "New Evidence on the Value of Financial Advice", The Investment Funds Institute of Canada, 2012: 15

If you start off with a negative net worth (meaning you owe more than you have in assets), don't be disappointed as this is a reality for many millennials as they exit school with accumulated student loan and tuition related debt. The goal here is to devise a debt repayment strategy. This may be an uncomfortable time for you, as many people hate having to deal with debt, but don't worry. Leaning on the right financial professional means not having to go through this phase alone.

During this debt repayment phase, you could lean on the following members of your financial power team, financial advisor, mortgage agent (if you already own real estate) credit specialist or banker. The goal here is to take your net worth from negative to at least "black" (meaning you don't owe anything, but you also haven't begun to accumulate any assets).

For example, your current net worth is in the negative at –$30,000 (point A) year over year, your goal is to see that –$30,000 reduce to perhaps –$20,000 the following year, then eventually –$10,000, 0, +$10,000 (point B) and so on and so on.

Changes don't happen overnight, but the little, daily, positive money habits that you can acquire will take you from point A to point B in no time.

According to Statistics Canada, the top 20% of income earners held 49% of household wealth, where the top 20% of income earners had a net worth of $1.8 million per household in 2017, compared to $214,000 for the bottom 20%. On average, those in the top income bracket earned $164,117 per household while those in the bottom income earned $26,513 per household. As for wealth, relatively more of Canada's household disposable income was concentrated in British Columbia in 2017[9].

So, it is important for us to keep in mind that the wealthy, based on the data above, don't focus on how much they make but rather their net worth. As you can see, net worth drives one's real wealth numbers, even though you can use income or money made to bolster your net worth. So a part of wealth building strategies we will also explore how one could effectively reduce debt while growing assets. We explore debt repayment strategies more thoroughly in the next chapter.

Millennial Money Journal Activity

Calculate Your Current Net Worth

Gather all your investment/savings statements as well as your debt statements, most of which you should be able to access online, if you don't have paper copies.

You can use the chart below to record your data and total your current net worth. (I know there are a lot of online programs that offer this service, but I find there is power in writing the information down on paper and really tracking it.)

---

[9] Statistics Canada. 2016. "Household income in Canada: Key results from the 2016 Census". Ottawa. Released Sept. 2017. Ottawa. https://www150.statcan.gc.ca/n1/daily-quotidien/170913/dq170913a-eng.htm

Assets	
Savings account	$2,000
RRSP	$5,300

Total Assets _____

Liabilities	
Car Loan	$4,200
Student Loan	$19,600

Total Assets _____

Net Worth	
Total Assets	
– Total Liabilities	
Net worth Total	

Building a positive net worth is the beginning step to leaving a positive legacy and building generational wealth. The key here is to ensure that you have truly cultivated a mindset for wealth or it is possible you may find yourself back at square one or in an even worse position than where you started.

It is important that the mindset discussed and you worked on in chapter 2 has been adopted and maintained because without it, you will likely face financial challenges that will induce you to stop rather than really pushing through for change.

If you desire massive wealth, it is important that, first, you believe that you have the power to become wealthy and that you are deserving of this wealth.

You wouldn't believe how many people attain massive levels of wealth and because of guilt or poor money management, they lose every single bit of money they had. A clear example of this is with lottery winners. Business Insider wrote an article chronicling some lottery winners who blew their winnings shortly after winning major sums (2.76 Million for one couple, 16.2 Million, 5 Million etc)[10]. Although this article is American, Canadians do share many similar characteristics to our American counterparts and this just highlights the importance of having a mindset for wealth that will help to encourage and foster ones financial success.

Something I would be remiss in discussing is the increased number of millennials who are betting on themselves by going into business for themselves. According to an economic report published by Royal Bank of Canada (RBC) the share of self employed individuals under 30 has doubled over the past two decades[11].

---

[10] Pamela Engel, "21 Lottery winners who blew it all," Business Insider, Jan. 6, 2016 https://www.businessinsider.com/lottery-winners-who-lost-everything-2016-1

[11] Laura Cooper, "Millennials", RBC Economics/Research, Oct. 2016, http://www.rbc.com/economics/economic-reports/pdf/other-reports/Millennials-October%202016.pdf

The mere fact that millennials are going into business for themselves at such a fast rate is an indication that millennials are already poised to control their earning power.

Although no one will argue the validity of knowing when and how much you get paid as an employee, it is much harder for employees to attain massive wealth from their salaries alone. This doesn't mean that it's impossible; you just have to acknowledge the increased difficulty of this happening.

The remarkable thing is millennials are diving into self employment at rapid rates by either contracting their services out to mega corporations or by starting and growing very lucrative side hustles (a term used to describe entrepreneurial efforts outside of their 9-5 jobs).

This means if you want to crush debt at a rapid rate, you have the power to do this. If you want to save for that dream home, you can you have infinite power to do amazing things, so it's up to you to make it happen.

So, what happens if you aren't an entrepreneur? Guess what? You still have power in your hands. You have the power to negotiate your salary, and I'm a huge proponent of employment tied to some form of bonus structure, either based on your personal performance or on the performance of the company you work for.

Early on in my career before I became a full time entrepreneur, I learned the power of always negotiating my salaries and even my starting wages. I was even successful in doing this when I worked in a unionized environment.

The following are some real life examples of tactics I used while working in corporate Canada.

Like I said, in my first real job where I received T4s and filed taxes at age 15 working at a shoe store, I remember the day very clearly. I was at the mall with my aunt (who is more like my sister because of our closeness in age) and we walked into this store and after chatting up to one of the sales reps and buying a pair of shoes I boldly said, "Are you guys hiring?" Unbeknownst to me at the time, the owner was the one at the register and he told me to come in the next Saturday to work (I guess I would prove myself on their busiest day), and we'd go from there.

I went in that Saturday, worked my butt off and sold a ton of shoes. After my shift was over, he went into the till and paid me for my day's work.

We began discussing my pay rate and hours. I was told my minimum wage would be $6.15/hour, the legal minimum wage in Ontario at the time because I was under sixteen. Right away, I began negotiating. I told him I would be agreeable to work only if, in addition to my hourly rate, he would pay me a commission. Guess what? He took the deal, and I felt amazing. Here I was, a 15 year old girl negotiating what would be my first "real" job, even if all I negotiated was a commission of ten cents per item sold. This was still a great lesson for me. I would always negotiate whatever someone was willing to pay me because ten cents per shoe was better in my pocket than in theirs.

Another example of my negotiating was during a time I was working at the bank, and like clockwork every year, it was time to negotiate my raise. I had already figured out what the inflation rate was (a continual increase in the price of goods and services) as defined by *Webster's Dictionary*, and I knew the average inflation rate was 3%, which determined my raise would need to be a minimum 3% + my merited raise for that year. I would always look at my sales numbers and targets and how I was able to meet or exceed sales goals and determine, based on performance, what I felt was an acceptable raise in my eyes.

In other words, unlike most employees, I went into these meetings prepared. I recall the first time I approached one of my managers during this negotiation phase; she was surprised that I didn't accept the raise she was offering. When I told her that the raise didn't even account for inflation, and I would be, in fact, working for free, she gave me a bit of a smile in agreement and admiration that I took the time to know this. She agreed and based on my performance thought I deserved a raise reflective of my work. We rescheduled our meeting for the next day, giving her time to review her budget, and I'm happy to say the next day I left her office with an acceptable raise and a deeper mutual respect between my manager and myself.

These are two examples of the many tactics I used over the years while I was an employee to ensure I got the most out of every employer I worked for. You'd be surprised how many people I know never prepare for their merit increase meetings and always accept the increase presented by their employer, which almost always is an increase less than or perhaps equal to inflation.

Do yourself a favour: know you are always in business for yourself. You owe it to yourself to learn the art of negotiating your merit increase or stating or expanding your side hustle into full-time entrepreneurism or you could be leaving big money on the table.

The key is to know what you are worth, so if you've put in the work and are deserving of a great raise don't be shy in demanding it. However, you have to be truthful to yourself if you are not deserving of a raise because your performance hasn't been the best. You need to soul search and figure out what is prohibiting you from performing at your highest level, even if that means you need to find a job that keeps you inspired and wanting to always give 100%.

I'm of the mindset that my income must grow into my goals rather than my goals shrinking into my income, and a sure way to accelerate this is by taking your pay into your own hands.

Dream big with me and make things happen.

Here, I've included a list of potential side hustles to build your income while you work your 9-5.

1. Provide graphic designing services
2. Become a local tour guide
3. Be a virtual assistant
4. Plan events
5. Salvage and sell antiques
6. Sell crafts online
7. Become a peer to peer taxi driver (*uber, lyft*)
8. Teach a musical instrument
9. Become a tutor

Got Debt?

Guess what, you're not alone.

According to Statistics Canada's, the average Canadian household owes $1.71 for every dollar of disposable income, which, year over year, has been trending up[12]. So, what does this mean? It simply means Canadians need to get a grip on our overall debt, and fast.

The interesting thing to note is that debt, in and of itself, is not something that happens overnight, so it is important to pinpoint the main cause for this increasing debt load and learn to change the behaviours that led you down the debt road in the first place. If when you track your spending, you realize that you have a cash flow problem, and you are spending on credit cards/lines of credits to maintain your basic lifestyle. You will have to make some serious adjustments to your overall spending.

Or if the debt has accumulated as a result of frivolous, unnecessary spending, you will need to re-evaluate your overall financial goals and commit to reining in the spending to make some serious headway when it comes to your overall financial success.

The truth is debt is the biggest obstacle between you and your dreams of wealth accumulation and the enemy to your income. It's the equivalent of throwing money in a "black hole" with no expectation of seeing that money again. So, it is imperative that you get a grip on it before it is too late.

---

[12] Pete Evans, "Canadians owe $1.71 for every dollar of disposable income they have, a new record high," CBC, Dec. 14, 2017 https://www.cbc.ca/news/business/debt-income-1.4448098

Here is one of the the greatest debt repayment strategy in my humble opinion; it is one that many of you are perhaps familiar with: "The Debt Snow ball Effect", originally coined and promoted by Dave Ramsey. The reason I believe in the Snowball Method is that, psychologically, people have success using this strategy because they see the debt disappear before their eyes, which helps to motivate them to stay on task and continue to plug away at their debt until it is fully eliminated.

The concept of the Snowball Effect is that you gather all your debt statements and organize them by dollar amount owed, smallest to largest (this is irrespective of the interest rate you are paying on these debts).

Once you've organized all your debt by smallest to largest outstanding, you write the amount of the minimum payment required for each debt. Also, take this time to review your no budget budget and prioritize debt repayments to the highest priority and, therefore, allocate all extra cash to the elimination of bad debt (all the while paying the minimum payments on all the debts), starting with the smallest debt amount until that is fully paid, and then focusing your energy on the next smallest debt until that is paid and so forth. The following example lists various credit products:

Credit card 1: balance $1,500; interest rate 19.99 (minimum payment $45/month)

Credit card 2: balance $650; interest rate 12.99% (minimum payment $19.50/month)

Line of credit: $4,500; interest rate 9.5% (minimum payment $135/month)

Car loan: $9,800; interest rate 4.99% (monthly payment $250)

Arrange debt the following way, itemized by outstanding dollar balance:

Credit card 2: balance $650; interest rate 12.99% (minimum $19.50/month)

Credit card 1: balance $1,500; interest rate 19.99% (minimum payment $45/month)

Line of credit: $4,500; interest rate 9.5% (minimum payment $135/month)

Car loan: $9,800; interest rate 4.99% (monthly payment $250)

So, let's say you review your no budget budget and discover you have an extra $120 per month that you can put towards debt.

Toward eliminating your debt, you would pay the minimums on all debts, but you would pay the additional $120/month to **credit card 2** (as this has the lowest outstanding balance and will be paid off much sooner than putting the $120 towards the highest interest debt) until that card is paid off, which should take approximately 5.5 months to accomplish in this example.

Once you've paid off **credit card 2**, you would then focus your attention on eliminating the debt on **credit card 1** (which is the next credit facility with the lowest balance owing) by continuing with the same strategy but instead of paying only an additional $120/month, you would be paying an additional $139.50/month, accounting for the minimum payment of $19.50, you are no longer required to pay on **credit card 2** because that card has been paid off.

To review, you would continue to make all minimum payments on all the debts but in addition to the minimum payment of $45 for **credit card 1**, you would be applying an additional $139.50/month until credit card 1 has been paid in full; this should take approximately 11 months to accomplish.

You can clearly see that using the snowball method has successfully "killed" 2 debts and this has all been accomplished in less than a year. It is clear how the snowball method psychologically promotes great money repayment because it keeps you motivated to stay on plan; the results are right before your eyes.

Unlike other debt repayment strategies that suggest you tackle debt by highest to lowest interest rate, the snow ball method focuses on paying debt based on lowest to highest dollar amount outstanding, because of the positive psychological effects it promotes as people are shown to stick to the plan at greater numbers as they see debts being paid in full[13].

Although, in theory, paying the highest interest debt off first makes the most sense financially, it has been shown that the level of success with this debt repayment strategy is not as successful as the snowball method because it is hard to stay motivated. People feel as though their debt will never go away because it's hard to see actual results, especially when the amount outstanding is large. Whereas, the snowball method begins showing signs of success early on, in most cases (depending on debt amounts and funds available to allocate to the debt) within six months or less[14].

The key to success here is to ensure you're paying down and "killing" this debt. Stop using your credit cards except when you can pay off the card in full before the lender's interest free grace period ends.

---

[13] Dave Ramsey, The Total Money Makeover (Nashville, TN: Nelson Books, 2013), 106

[14] Dave Ramsey, The Total Money Makeover (Nashville, TN: Nelson Books, 2013), 107

Remember, if you can't pay for it in "cash" ("cash" meaning anything other than on credit), you can't afford it.

Millennial Money Journal Activity

So, now, I invite you to take action by gathering all your current debt statements and, like the example laid out, organize all your debt from smallest to largest balance owing.

Write out the minimum payments for all debts, and then visit your no budget budget to determine if you have any additional money available to put towards your debt each month, if you do, you would employ the "Snow Ball Method" described earlier to begin your debt repayment strategy.

I might add that you shouldn't beat yourself up if after you've worked the numbers, you discover you don't have any extra funds to put towards these debts other than maintaining the minimum payment required. What I would recommend in this instance is that you commit to putting all "windfall" forms of cash towards these debts (windfall refers to money given to you that is above and beyond your regular monthly income). Windfalls could be bonuses, income tax refunds, birthday/holiday gifts etc.

All that is left here is for you to implement the plan and keep on it until you've eventually paid all your debt in full.

Debt Snow Ball		
Credit Type	Balance	min. payment
Credit Card	$500	$10
Line of Credit	$2,500	$25

Time to Save

Invest your "coins" and build your own "money bag"

Now that you have a game plan when it comes to your debt repayment, it's important for us to shift our gears and look at opportunities to save and invest your money outside of the "paying yourself" strategy discussed earlier in the book.

I am a huge fan of always tapping into experts and this would be the perfect time to enlist the assistance of a trusted financial advisor. Remember, even though this is your plan, you don't have to go at it alone.

To recap quickly, you should have already started to put aside a percentage of all income. Again, the recommendation is that you put aside 10% of all income. I say start off with a percentage that is comfortable for you as this may all be new to you, and it's important that as you build the "savings muscle," you don't get discouraged and stop this plan altogether. If that means you are saving 2% or 5% of every paycheque, it's better than saving nothing at all. As soon as you become comfortable with this new habit, you can review your percentages and increase accordingly.

Another key to the success of this paying yourself method is to make the savings automated wherever possible, by taking the transfers out of your hands as this will help to ensure that transfers will happen continually without issue.

A question/statement I typically get from my self employed clients is "I don't get paid regularly, and I don't know what my income will be from month to month." My suggestion here is to use last year's income figures to gauge the expected income and work the savings in as though it is a debt payment, meaning you have an obligation to meet that payment as you would be obligated to paying rent and, therefore, ensuring you're putting this money away.

For example, let's say that last year you grossed $72,000. If you decided to put aside 5% of your gross income, you would need to include a monthly "pay yourself" bill payment of $300. You could then review every quarter how your income is trending and adjust to reflect the income you are, in fact, receiving.

We also previously discussed saving 3–6 months' worth of expenses for an emergency fund. You should be actively setting aside money into your emergency fund until you've achieved this goal. This may mean saving 2.5% into your "pay yourself" account, with the other 2.5% going into your emergency fund until this goal is achieved. Once you've built up your emergency fund, you can then put the full 5% into paying yourself.

So, after you've saved up your emergency fund, you can begin to explore other investment/savings strategies.

Here is where your financial advisor will help uncover what matters the most to you.

For a moment, I want you to visualize some of your financial goals, goals you want to achieve in the next 3–5 years, in 5–7 years, and 7–10 years.

Examples:

3–5 years: be free of consumer debt

3–5 years: purchase first home

5–7 years: purchase investment property

7–10 years: accumulate a "cash-like" portfolio of $250,000 (savings deposits, government treasuries, savings bonds etc., anything that is easy to be converted into cash at any time).

Millennial Money Journal Activity

Now, take the time to write down some of your financial goals.

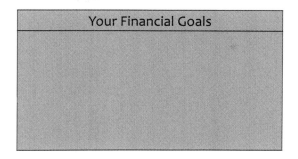

With that completed, you can see why it's super important to have a financial advisor to devise a plan for you to achieve these goals.

The major activity I will have you do here is interview three financial advisors and hire one. Believe me, you will thank me for this sooner rather than later. It has been shown that "advised households have 4.2 times assets as non advised households" It has also been shown that "advice improves savings behaviour"[15]. So, the key as you can see is finding the best advisor for you. I would start by asking for recommendations from trusted colleagues or family and friends. Gather reviews, set an appointment and interview them, use the same questions introduced earlier as a starting point to see if their style and energy complements your own and if it does, get started on implementing a plan.

---

[15] Jon Cockerline, "New Evidence on the Value of Financial Advice", The Investment Funds Institute of Canada, 2012: 9

Millennials and Real Estate

Homeowner at 21. What?

We've heard countless times how real estate has helped create many millionaires within North America, so it should be no surprise that the vast majority of millennials would also want to replicate this success with real estate.

I became a homeowner at 21, four months before my 22nd birthday, and although for many this may seem young, I knew early on that if I devised a strategy and worked with professionals, in no time my boyfriend (now my husband) and I would be able to achieve our goal of home ownership.

Let me be real and give you the backstory of my home ownership plan. Although my mother and I have an amazing relationship now, I can admit I was a brat who often overlooked all the sacrifices she made in order to provide not only for me, my sister, and brother but also for my three cousins she helped raise for ten years. It wouldn't be until I was an adult with my first daughter that I would truly appreciate my mother and her efforts. I guess motherhood gave me a fresh pair of lenses, and I'm thankful I was able to build the amazing relationship I now have with my mom.

The thing is, my mom was a homeowner; she saved and sacrificed to purchase her first home on her own (previous townhouse in Galloway was purchased by both my mom and grandmother) in Ajax, Ontario. This was a huge accomplishment for my mom. But what sometimes happens is people get so caught up with the monthly mortgage payment that they forget that there are a whole lot of other expenses needed to run and maintain a household. For example, heat, water, lights, lawn care, furnace and appliance maintenance, etc., especially when you're single caring for six children. To say reality hit my mom with a ton of bricks is an understatement. Even though she previously owned a home with my grandmother, that house was a revolving door for people always staying to get themselves together. Though I wouldn't consider that house a boarding house with multiple tenants sharing expenses, it sure had elements of this; money typically flowed from one person or another.

Now my mom was on her own. The only money coming in was from her biweekly paycheque. My mom did not receive financial support from my father, or from anyone. It is almost hard to believe that my mom lasted as long as she did in her home without the financial support needed to maintain it and her family. My mom, feeling short of options, began to put blind trust in people, and when her bills began to pile up and banks and creditors started to call, she did as she was advised to do: take on more debt than she could manage to "Bandaid" her situation. This didn't help her get to the root of the problem, and in no time, it became apparent that my mom would have to sell her home, or she would lose it under "power of sale" (when the lender will sell the property in the event of default). Just like that, my mom sold the house, and that is when I decided I would move on with my life (ouch, not so nice when I reflect back now). To me, my mom didn't know how to manage money, and everything around her was more chaotic than I could manage. Yes, I know now I was selfish and never recognized the sacrifices my mom made for her family, but I was super concerned with how my life was being affected and could care less about my family as a whole. At the time, I was 19 years old and didn't want to bother with the headaches and responsibilities my mom was facing as I felt she caused them on herself (but boy do I know better now).

So, at 19, I moved in with my boyfriend (now my husband) and his uncle, in his uncle's condo. We pretty much had the freedom to do what we wanted as his uncle only slept at the condo and was hardly home for us to feel like we were inconveniencing him.

It wouldn't be long until I started to watch those for sale signs to become intrigued by the possibility of moving out and getting our own space. I approached my boyfriend and said, "I think we should get our own apartment." I figured we could afford it (at the time I was in school full time but also working a steady 30–35 hours/week, and he was working full time at Merrill Lynch).

He shot my idea down without hesitation. In not so many words, he told me my idea was crazy and that the only way he would move from where we were at (remember, we could do what we wanted at his uncle's place where we weren't really paying "rent") would be if we moved into our own place.

A light bulb went off, and I was, like, OK, we will get our own place, no problem.

It didn't take long for me to realize that we could carry a mortgage, but we didn't want to leave ourselves "house poor," so we decided to use a strategy we saw our friend's mother use for her duplex after she went through her divorce (she occupied one part of the home and rented the other part of the home).

We quickly asked for references and hired a real estate agent as well as a mortgage broker. We told them our grand plan, and we began our journey. In no time, we were able to secure a home that, funnily enough, was under a "power of sale" by CIBC. We planned to live upstairs (3 bedrooms) and rent the basement (studio apartment).

We got our financing approved. The lender called our employers to have all our conditions for the mortgage approved, but fate would have it that in a few days of closing the deal, my boyfriend lost his job. I kid you not.

We felt like this was a crazy joke being played on us and because we released all conditions with our sale (having met bank conditions and signed off on the inspection of the home), we were now contractually obligated to close on the deal, so there was no turning back. We began praying that the lender wouldn't have any other reason to call my boyfriend's employer, CIBC, as they had bought out Merrill Lynch, because we knew if they called them again, we would be screwed. Thankfully, because they had already verified employment, there was no need for them to call again.

Quickly, we realized how blessed we were in deciding to buy a duplex because we knew the rental income would come in handy for our mortgage payments.

With all these changes happening to us so fast, we decided to switch our game plan and rent upstairs (3 bedrooms), leaving us to occupy the basement studio apartment. This became such a financially lucrative deal that, over the years, when we could have moved upstairs, we decided not to as we quickly realized the cash flow we made was great.

That very first year, with my husband having lost his full time job and me working and going to school, we never once had to make a mortgage payment as the rental income from upstairs covered it all, including utilities. All we had to pay was property taxes.

So, imagine here you have a 21 and a 24 year old owning a home, building equity, and living off of the rental income and only having to pay over $1,900/year in property taxes or $158/mth. Let's just say this was when we realized that real estate was definitely the way to go, and we became walking billboards and mouthpieces to anyone who would listen to the importance of investing in real estate.

I tell you this story as inspiration. I know times have changed, and it has become increasingly difficult for millennials to enter the real estate market recently, but I truly believe that with proper planning, you can achieve this goal, no problem. You may need to be creative and think outside the box, but with the right team and motivation I know you can achieve this goal.

Set the Goal, Plan and Execute You Can Own Real Estate Too

There is countless information that shows millennials are finding it increasingly difficult to enter the real estate market, but this should not be used as an excuse not to attempt it for yourself. The reality is that even though it is more difficult for millennials than baby boomers, (as illustrated earlier in the book). Millennials are still entering the real estate market; they are just having to become more creative with the solutions to their current challenges.

Millennials, now more than ever, are leaning on the support of family to make home ownership viable. In 2017 CBC published an article where they looked at an HSBC poll of millennials globally (including 10000 Canadians) that found that "More than a third of millennials surveyed, or 37 per cent, said they had made a withdrawal from the "bank of mom and dad" to cover housing costs. As well, 21 per cent of them hit up their parents to help them pay for other unexpected costs after they had purchased homes"[16].

---

[16] Pete Evans, "37% of young homeowners borrow from 'bank of mom and dad,' HSBC survey indicates," CBC, Feb. 28, 2017, https://www.cbc.ca/news/business/hsbc-housing-survey-1.4002458

This just shows that millennials are still looking to enter the real estate market, they may just take a bit longer with the planning phase, which means they might be living at home a bit longer than those of past decades and parents/family members are also stepping up in large rates to assist with their down payments and related closing cost. There has even been an increase of millennials choosing to stay at home and getting into real estate as investors first (this allows them to partner with other family members or friends) giving them the option of being invested without the pressure of finding 100% of the down payment themselves and qualifying for the mortgage themselves.

Another strategy that is becoming more and more common in recent times in the Greater Vancouver and Greater Toronto Area's is "real estate speed dating." The premise is that individuals pool their resources together with total strangers who have a similar goal of home ownership and the desire to live without the need to sacrifice their wish list. They enter this arrangement from an "investors" perspective but instead of renting the home out the buyers would occupy the home together making them roommates with investor interest in the property[17].

Any of these strategies may or may not work for you. The key is you always want to be open to the possibility of entering the market, even if your path looks significantly different for you than it does for someone else. The key is to simply research options and enter through the means that makes the most sense for you.

---

[17] Erica Vella, "Would you buy a house with a stranger? Toronto real estate speed dating a new option," Global News, May 5, 2017, https://globalnews.ca/news/3429209/would-you-buy-a-house-with-a-stranger-toronto-real-estate-speed-dating-a-new-option/

The following are the steps I take with my clients when they approach me with wanting to enter the real estate market. I get everyone to go through what is called a Home Buying Plan that helps to prequalify clients, to assess where they currently stand financially. I devise a plan to encourage them and keep them accountable until they make that purchase.

It is my experience that 30–40% of first-time home buyers that come to me are ready immediately to enter the housing market while the other 60–70% require anywhere from 9–15 months to get themselves organized and make things happen. The good thing is I will always work with you no matter what stage you are at, and positive results always come for those willing to put in the work.

Here is a checklist I send to clients to help them get prepared for the homeownership conversation:

Millennial Money Journal Activity

Gather the following items, and, as a bonus, if you email the following documents to admin@mortgagesbynik.com, you will be given a free assessment and pre-qualification certificate, along with items to improve the strength of your application (if necessary).

- Proof of income, e.g. (two of your most recent pay stubs, letter of employment, T4, two of your most recent Notice of Assessments (what you get back from Revenue Canada once you've filed your taxes)
- A copy of your credit status (obtain one from a credit bureau, which will allow me to see

your credit status and advise you on improvements needed)
- Investment statements (to show where the source(s) of the down payment will come from if the down payment will come from them)
- Debt statements (all credit card bills, lines of credit, loan statements etc.)

The goal here is to tap into your power teamwork with a trusted mortgage agent/broker as well as trusted real estate agent as part of your real estate goals and strategy to make your goal of home ownership a reality.

REAL ESTATE GOALS

Millennial Money Journal Activity

Write out your real estate goals. Don't be shy. These goals could include the purchase of a principal residence, investment property, vacation home etc.
Dream Big!

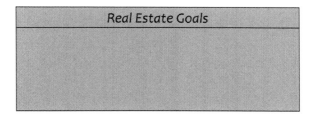

You'd Better Know Your Why

What will keep you motivated?

Truth is, we all deviate from time to time from our goals at hand. The idea is not to deviate too far from the plan that it becomes increasingly harder to get back on track. I would be lying if I didn't admit that there have been many times that I did not do things I know I should have or when I spent more than I should have. We have all taken that trip, bought that bag, or accepted a job that you know paid less than you deserved or worked somewhere you were "over" qualified for. However, all of these situations serve as reminders that we are all human, and no matter your level of financial success, we all, from time to time, have to re-focus ourselves and remind ourselves why sticking to our plan is bigger than fulfilling a temporary emotional need to indulge.

This is why it is super important to tap into your why; your why is your guiding force that will help to propel you into greatness and give you motivation when you feel you want to give up. Your why injects passion into your work and gives you a sense of purpose to get the things done even in moments when you don't feel like it. Without purpose and a plan, you may find that you've come up with a plan that you are not willing or motivated to work toward.

"Dreams don't work unless you do" (John C. Maxwell)

So, it is imperative for you to discover and unlock your "why." For many, their why can be their children, their church or religious organization, a feeling of never wanting to be poor again, or even to prove someone wrong (I never like focusing on what I don't want or on the negative, but a lot of people are driven by proving naysayers wrong), it is very possible to have multiple whys or even know that your why can change as your life goes through different shifts. The important thing is you need to identify in every moment what your why is, and your why needs to be bigger than you and something you hold with such regard that you would be willing to do anything to ensure your goals are met to align with the achievement of your why.

Currently, my biggest why's are

- My children (to leave a legacy for my children's children and creating generational wealth)

To be a giant giver

"you can't help the poor if you're one of them…" (Jay Z)

I need to have more than enough because I cannot give from what I do not have. I am super inspired by the Bill and Melinda Gates Foundation. The founders Bill and Melinda Gates are billionaires who have pledged to give away most of their wealth through their foundation. They are an amazing example of using their wealth for good and a reminder that money is a tool, and we are the ones who control the tool, so it's important that we always have a pure heart when dealing with money. Bill and Melinda Gates believe "that by giving people the tools to lead healthy, productive lives, we can help them lift themselves out of poverty".[18]

My last why is Li'l Nik (to show my little girl inside) and all little girls growing up and living in inner cities, that all things are possible when we have a dream, believe in it, and really put in the work. The world will have no choice but to materialize it.

Millennial Money Journal" Activity

Let's discover your "why."

You will want to start by asking yourself the following questions.

1. What makes you come alive? What puts "fire" in your belly and is bigger than you and connects you to what you are passionate about?
2. What are your strengths? And where do you add the most value to those around you and your community at large?
3. What matters the most to you that when you look back on your life you will be proud of?
4. It's also important to know "how" you work because this will allow you to live your best why.

Once you've discovered your why, it's important to share it with others. This is important in so many ways. The universe will begin to hear you and respond to make things happen for you. Sharing your why also offers

---

[18] Bill Gates and Melinda Gates, "Who we are: Letter from Bill and Melinda Gates," Gates Foundation, https://www.gatesfoundation.org/Who-We-Are/General-Information/Letter-from-Bill-and-Melinda-Gates, link accessed Oct. 12, 2018

inspiration to those around you. I find there is nothing more amazing than people who know what they want in life and are willing to do all that is necessary to make it happen. So, you don't know who you may be inspiring with your new discovery, so share, share, share.

Email me your "why" at info@mrsmoneybaggs.com. Let's start a conversation, and I will become your champion in ensuring you move towards your why and ensure you don't deviate from achieving your financial goals.

Stay on Course

How to remain motivated and stick to your plan

So, now that you have your why, it's important for you to stick to the plan. Again, the plan is not supposed to be rigid but to flow as life changes. You may start off with your goal of paying off your student loan, and in 2–3 years, your new goal may be to purchase your first home. Once you've achieved those goals, you may want to amass a wealth of "X" amount.

Currently, I'm working on my next goal: to purchase a multiunit (10 units or more) building. Like you, I have my goal. I need to develop a plan and make it happen. We don't stop until the goal is achieved.

My ultimate longterm goal is to be a billionaire.

"…bet before I go I put a billion on the board" (Jay Z).

"Millennial Money Journal" Activity:

Let's recap and rewrite your Financial Goals
1–3year Financial Goals

_____
_____
_____

3–5year Financial Goals

_____
_____
_____

5–10year Financial Goals

_____
_____
_____

10+ year Financial Goals

_____
_____
_____

Conclusion

It is my prayer that something in this guide has blessed you and has given you the motivation to get started on building your own wealth. This guide is just that, a guide, so use what you find useful and disregard all the rest because my exact journey may not work for you, but I'm certain bits and pieces of it may.

Again, complete all the Millennial Money Journal activities and be sure to email me to let me know what your number one financial goal is and what you plan on implementing today to ensure you achieve this goal. Use the guide to think about this and know I am here to be a resource to keep you motivated along the way.

Be sure to let me know what you think of the book and stay in touch I'm social so follow and tag us with your purchase as we will be running some amazing contest for our social followers.

Facebook	/mrsmoneybaggs
Instagram	@mrsmoneybaggs_
Twitter	@mrsmoneybaggs
Website	mrsmoneybaggs.com
Email	info@mrsmoneybaggs.com
Telephone	1.877.207.7204

About Me

Nicolle Williams' mission is to educate and inspire millennials to gain financial empowerment so they can live their best life.

Since 2003, she has worked in Canada's financial sector, from financial advisor to her current role as a mortgage agent.

Her passion for financial literacy and education has garnered the attention of her peers and community, having been awarded the prestigious "100 Black Women to Watch in Canada" by CIBWE in 2016 and "150 'HERstory in Black', black women who have made a place in Canadian History" by CBC in 2017.

She is the host and creator of "Money Tube," a popular YouTube channel that empowers today's millennials by "helping them to walk into their financial destiny."

She is also the co-creator of "Money Boss Up," a financial academy offering intensive workshops that work directly with millennials to push them to achieve their financial goals in an intimate, educational environment.

More than a motivational speaker, mentor, and financial literacy advocate, Nicolle is a wife, mother, and daughter of the most High.

Made in the USA
Middletown, DE
25 June 2019